# P.D. (Puppy Dog) BROWN
## Learns How To Fly

Written by
Karl Niemiec

Illustrated by
Alice Niemiec

# For our kids
# because we love them.

# P.D. (Puppy Dog) Brown

Copyright © 2011

Karl J. Niemiec
Alice Niemiec
LapTopPublishing.com
A Paperless Press

P.O. Box 3501 Carmel, IN 46082

**ISBN: 978-0-9833663-7-9**

A book about the
inspirational powers
behind encouraging
friends and family
to fulfill their
lifelong dreams.

Once upon a time, in a
magical town with a beach,
lived an adventurous puppy named
P.D. (Puppy Dog) Brown.

One sunny day, P.D. Brown looked up to the sky, saw seagulls floating in the breeze and said to himself, "I believe I can learn to fly."

On his way to learn how, P.D. stopped to ask Mr. Gray Cat's advice, because Mr. Gray knew lots of dogs and birds.

"Oh my, a flying puppy dog," said Mr. Gray Cat. "I was once chased by a Bird Dog, you know. So anything is possible. Say, I just spied Mrs. Pigeon. Ask her, she's taught flocks of birds."

"What a great idea," P.D. said.
"Thank you, Mr. Gray, I'll do that."

"You'd be a Puppy Fly," cooed Mrs. Pigeon.

"So, you can teach me to be one?" P.D. asked.

"Well, we birds just wing it," she said. "But I believe in you, P.D. Brown. You're a brave pup. So find your wind, and let it lift your spirits."

"Okay, I believe I can wing it. I'm a Puppy Fly."

"Spread those ears, P.D. and I'll see you in the sky."

So, P.D. Brown jumped for the wind until he sat out of breath at Mr. Chipmunk's ponies-go-round.

"I've seen horseflies and butterflies. Surely the wind has enough strength for a Puppy Fly," Mr. Chipmunk said.

"But the best wind is up so high. How will I get up there to catch it?" P.D. asked.

Mr. Chipmunk scratched his head. "Just keep your head up and your eyes open."

"Okay, thank you, I will. I'll find that wind and I'll be a Puppy Fly."

"That a boy, Puppy Dog Brown. May that wind give you flight."

P.D. ran down to the beach.

"Mrs. Crab? Are you here?" he yelled.

"Yes, P.D., you're sitting on my head."

"Oh, sorry, Mrs. Crab."

"You want to fly up there? Well, let's see," Mrs. Crab said. "I've sung Shoo Fly, and I've snapped at a housefly. Why shouldn't there be a Puppy Fly, if that's truly what you want to be?"

"You mean it's possible?"

"Why sure. When the time comes, seize the moment, and give it all you've got."

"Thank you. I'll hang on with all my might," P.D. Brown replied.

"Good luck, P.D. Brown."

So on his way down to the golden beach he found the hardworking Mr. Turtle.

"Oh hi, P.D. Brown. Rumor has it you're wanting to fly."

"I believe I can learn how if given a shot."

"Well, you just may be in luck today, Puppy Fly. Take a look up there."

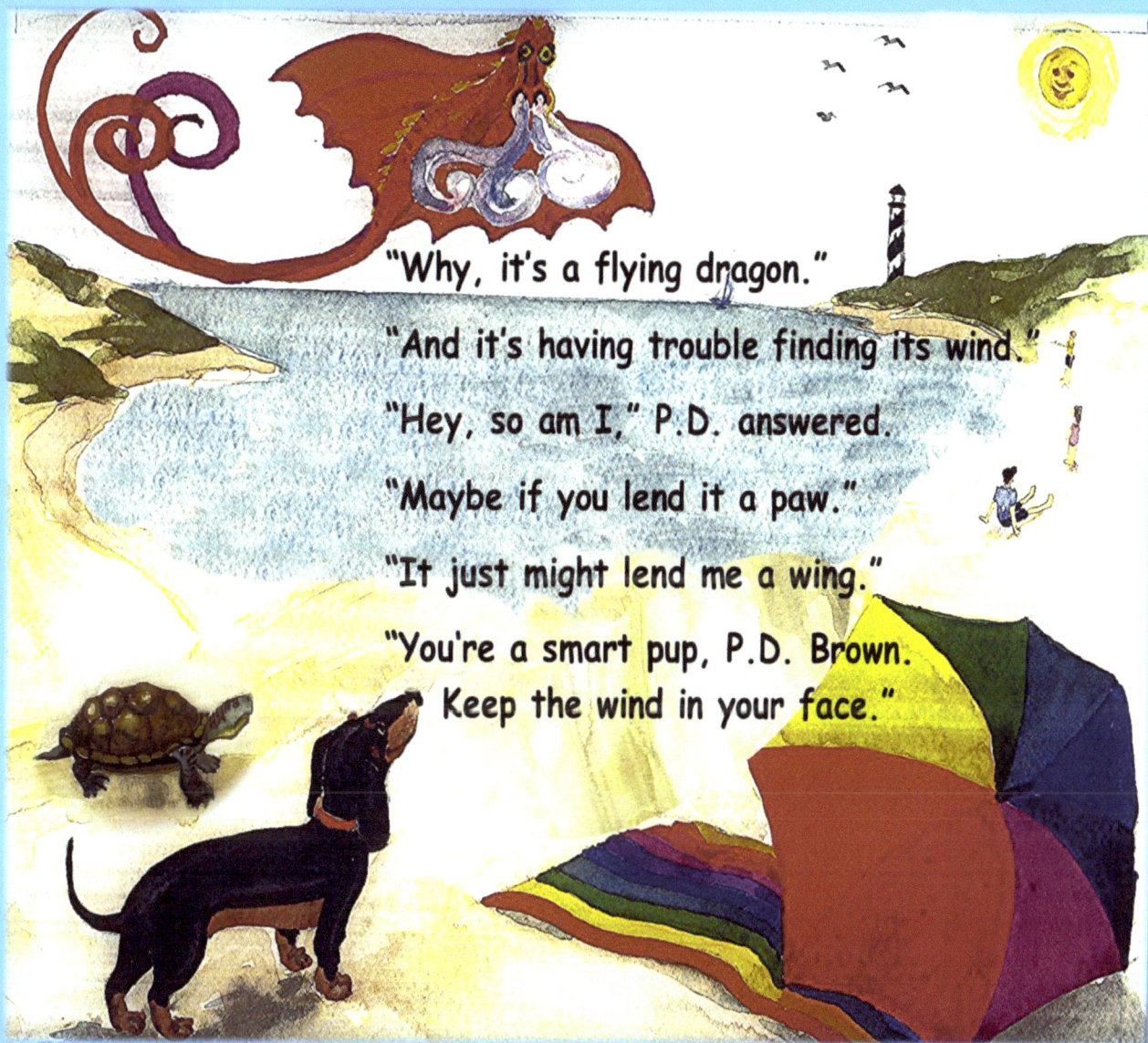

"Why, it's a flying dragon."

"And it's having trouble finding its wind."

"Hey, so am I," P.D. answered.

"Maybe if you lend it a paw."

"It just might lend me a wing."

"You're a smart pup, P.D. Brown. Keep the wind in your face."

Suddenly, the little girl yelled,
"Oh no, I lost the dragon's string!"

So, into the wind P.D. dashed.
Remembering all the encouragements.
"If I lend a paw I believe it's possible
to wing it, by keeping my head up and
seizing the moment to fly," P.D. said.

"Look, it's P.D.," yelled the boy!

"He's come to the rescue," answered their father.

His family and friends
laughed and applauded.

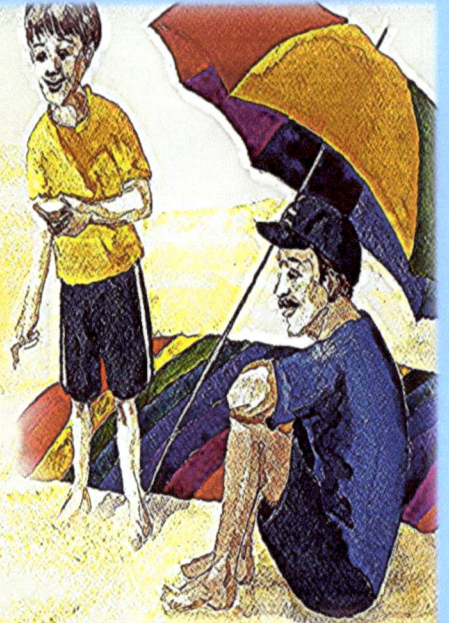

As they all watched
P.D. (Puppy Dog) Brown
turn into a real Puppy Fly.

On his way over the ocean,
P.D. smiled at Mrs. Pigeon,
waved at Mr. Chipmunk,
and winked at Mrs. Crab.
He hung on with all his might,
as he pointed his ears and
just winged it.

When the wind gave up the boy gave P.D. Brown a great big hug.

"That was incredible," the little girl said.

So, they all plopped down to share treats until their father said, "Let's go home and tell Mom that our P.D. Brown truly learned to fly today."

So, it took most of the day, but with encouragements from all his family and friends, P.D. (Puppy Dog) Brown was proud to report to Mr. Gray Cat that he was a real Puppy Fly.

"That's great," P.D., Mr. Gray Cat said. "We all knew you'd find a way."

So in the end,
encouragements from friends and family
were as magical as dragons.

And helped this puppy dog learn to fly!

www.ingramcontent.com/pod-product-compliance
Lightning Source LLC
Chambersburg PA
CBHW042110040426
42448CB00002B/207